D1550429

LAST WISHES

A Funeral Planning Manual and Survivors Guide

LAST WISHES

A Funeral Planning Manual and Survivors Guide

Malcolm James & Victoria Lynn

MAVAMI, INC.
Valley Forge, PA

Publisher's Cataloging-in -Publication Data
 (Provided by Quality Books, Inc.)

James, Malcolm, 1956-
     Last wishes : a funeral planning manual and
survivor's guide / Malcolm James and Victoria Lynn. -- 1st
ed.
     p. cm.
     Includes index.
     ISBN 0-9704853-0-1

     1.   Funeral rites and ceremonies--United States--
Planning. 2. Death--Social aspects. 3. Death--
Psychological aspects. 4. Bereavement. I. Lynn,
Victoria, 1957- II. Title.

GT3203.J36 2000   393'.0973
                                   QBI00-901507

ACKNOWLEDGEMENTS

A sincere thank-you to our family and friends who have reviewed and made recommendations to improve this book. To our children, Alexandra and Mitchell for their understanding and cooperation in the development of this endeavor, Last Wishes - A Funeral Planning Manual and Survivors Guide.

CONTENTS

FROM THE AUTHORS

Thank you for purchasing this manual. It was created for you and your survivors, and our goal is that you, your family and friends will benefit from the documents included.

This manual was written to address the void often left when a loved one dies and the family and friends make final arrangements with little or no knowledge of what the deceased's *Last Wishes* were. This manual covers all aspects of pre-planning your funeral, but it will also assist your survivors at the appropriate time.

All too often people leave a funeral service and comment that this was not what their loved one would have wanted: she would have wanted azaleas, he would have wanted Mozart.

Your funeral does not have to end that way. You can pre-plan your funeral so that it is clear what you would want. First and foremost, you envision a peaceful and dignified end to your life without additional pain or suffering for your loved ones. You do not wish to place unnecessary burdens on your family or friends at a time when they need support the most.

Our experience upon the death of our father prompted us to prepare this book. In April 1997 our father died. Our parents had been living in Florida for a number of years, enjoying their retirement. Suddenly with no warning, our father, who was a relatively healthy man of seventy-one years, suffered a massive heart attack and died in his sleep.

Our family pulled together in our time of need. Of course, our mother was upset to lose her husband of over fifty years. The love and support of her children helped to sustain her, but at the time she thought that all of the funeral decisions were going to be easy since ten years earlier they had pre-planned their funerals. Through a program at their church in Upstate New York, each had completed a pre-planning questionnaire regarding their funeral preferences.

After many phone calls, our mother finally reached the church office in her hometown. She tearfully expressed the news that her husband had died and asked for a copy of the funeral planning forms that they had completed so many years before. Unfortunately, the church secretary knew nothing of the pre-planning forms. When she was unable to help, our mother spoke with the minister, but he too was unable to assist her, explaining that he had been recently assigned to this particular church, and had never heard about nor seen any funeral pre-planning forms. Although, extremely compassionate, the minister recommended that our mother contact the local clergy to assist her with the funeral arrangements.

Our mother was beside herself and confused, as there were so .many issues to consider when planning a funeral service. Could she possibly remember what her husband's wishes were? Could she make decisions that he would have appreciated? What were his *Last Wishes*? Fortunately, she had her children with her at that time, drawing strength from them. With the assistance of the funeral director, local minister, florist, choral director and her family, the important decisions were made, but even with all that support our mother still had doubts. This experience proved to be a catalyst for this book and we thought that it was a great idea to pre-plan for your own funeral.

Each of us has the right to take control and to plan for our final ceremony and make the individual choices that will fully reflect our lifetime of experiences. This manual will guide you through that process.

Most decisions about purchasing funeral goods and services are made by people who are grieving and are under time constraints. Pre-planning helps you to make informed and thoughtful decisions about your funeral arrangements and also allows you to choose the specific items that you want and need. Pre-planning provides time to compare prices and offerings by one or more funeral providers. Additional benefits of pre-planning include:

- individuals can make their own choices,
- you can take personal control of your funeral decisions,
- fewer burdens on your family and friends,
- family and friends may move beyond the hectic funeral preparations to deal with their grief,
- reduced expenditures for your funeral,
- will make everyone aware of your *Last Wishes*.

While this manual will guide you in pre-planning your own funeral, there are certain circumstances when it will not replace other expert advice. <u>Last Wishes - A</u>

<u>Funeral Planning Manual and Survivors Guide</u> is not intended to replace the advice of a funeral director. If you have not yet chosen one, please refer to the Appendix in the back of this manual. The Appendix lists the various organizations that can help you contact a reputable funeral director. *Last Wishes* is not intended to replace your attorney who can help you prepare your *Last Will and Testament, Living Will, Power of Attorney* and other legal documents. State laws govern the legality of these documents. If you need an attorney, the local American Bar Association can refer you to an attorney who specializes in estates.

After speaking with your funeral director and attorney, you may still want to seek the advice and support of your clergy, friends and family about your *Last Wishes*.

We hope that this manual is helpful to you and that it will help you record your *Last Wishes*. We wish you the best of luck with your pre-planning. Our *Last Wish* is that you enjoy your life and try not to worry about what is to come some day. At the very least you have prepared and you have accomplished something with your very special life. Be proud and happy about that. We *Wish* you all the very best!

In order for this manual to assist in pre-planning for your funeral, it is recommended that you read each chapter in succession in order to gain an understanding of what you may want to include in your *Last Wishes and survivors guide*.

Why Pre-Plan, Chapter 3, will help you understand the importance of pre-planning your funeral and how this manual, Last Wishes A Funeral Planning Manual and Survivors Guide was developed. It is our hope that this chapter will help eliminate any doubt that you may have as to the importance of funeral pre-planning.

Funeral Practices, Chapter 4, describes the different types of funerals and religious ceremonies available. This chapter will help you to formulate ideas and assist you as you make decisions for your own funeral.

Completing The Forms, Chapter 5, includes detailed instructions for completing the *Last Wishes* forms. This chapter will help you put your decisions onto a format that will be easily read and understood by your survivors.

The Appendix, Chapter 6, includes a listing of business, professional and consumer groups that may provide more specific information. The Appendix will also offer selections of Biblical readings, flowers and their associated meaning, poems, hymns, secular and non-secular musical selections appropriate for a funeral ceremony.

The Glossary, Chapter 7, lists the terms used within the manual. The glossary is an alphabetical list of the terms with their respective definitions in plain, layman's English.

The Forms, Chapter 8, includes the forms to document your *Last Wishes*. Before completing this section, you should decide whether or not to include your loved ones or your executor in the decision making process of your *Last Wishes*.

As you proceed, keep in mind that as you grow older and as years pass, many of your choices may reflect your changing attitudes toward the world around you. We suggest that you keep your completed *Last Wishes* forms in a safe, but convenient place in order to make updates and changes as needed. If your *Last Wishes* forms are locked away in a safe deposit box, you may be inclined to ignore them, or forget they exist. In addition, many states will prohibit access to materials in a safe deposit box until after your funeral has taken place. This would defeat your intentions of making key decisions regarding your funeral arrangements.

Take the time to complete this manual in the comfort of your own home, discuss your ideas and wishes with your loved ones. Remember if you take the necessary steps to prepare for the last ceremony of life now while you can, it will ease the inevitable stress and eventual burden on your loved ones.

Pre-planning is preparation for an event or an occurrence that you know is going to take place before it actually happens.

Most of us do not know very much about funerals or the delicate process involved in planning and conducting a funeral. What we know about funerals is usually based on the funerals that we have attended or have seen on television or at the movie theater. We do not learn about funeral planning in school. Unless one of our relatives worked in a funeral parlor, we never learned anything in our homes about planning funerals either. It is a fact of life that most of us never learn enough about funerals until it is too late. Unfortunately, when a death occurs, it usually catches people unprepared.

No one really wants to talk about death or funerals, much less plan for their own funeral. Hey, call your friends up and invite them over this Saturday night for a funeral pre-planning party. I know what you are thinking. Who wants to talk about that? I'm still young. I still have my health. I still have plenty of time to plan for my funeral. If you have not pre-planned your funeral before your death, your family and friends will be making arrangements without any input from you.

Making prior plans and arrangements for your own funeral is an act of love, displaying your loving concern for those that you hold dear. Pre-planning eases the burdens placed upon your family and friends at a most tumultuous time in their lives. The decisions required in making funeral arrangements immediately after a loved one dies often leaves family members distraught and confused. Even seemingly simple choices become a source of tremendous frustration and doubt. What music should be played? What type of flowers should surround the casket? What readings should be given? Who should be notified? Pre-planning will not eliminate the sorrows that your family and friends feel at the time of your death, but it will help as they deal more comfortably and confidently with the process. Pre-planning will help them gain closure and move ahead with their lives.

A common misconception in funeral practice is that the ceremony must conform to church or family traditions. If you wish to have a funeral service that is different, feel free to be creative. The old proverb, funerals are for the living may be true, but you are entitled to have your *Last Wishes* respected. After all, it is your funeral, it is a celebration of your life and it should consist of your *Last Wishes*.

We wondered why most people failed to pre-plan for their funeral. Many of us plan our daily, weekly or monthly schedules. We know when we are scheduled to see the doctor. We know when we have to go to work or pick up our children from school. We know most of the mundane things that must and will occur during the course of our lives, yet we fall short when it comes to planning for our own funeral.

Have you ever gone on a vacation? Maybe you flew to the coast, or drove to Florida in the family van. How did it happen? Was it a spur of the moment decision or did you plan in advance? Did you have to let your employer know when you were going? What about money, did you save before you went? It takes careful pre-planning and perseverance to make a vacation become a memory that will last forever.

Have you ever been involved in a wedding or attended a wedding? Have you ever gone to a wedding where the bride or groom picks the church the wedding is to be held in? Let's talk about the freshly cut roses, carnations, and the other flowers that adorn the church or cathedral. Have you ever gone to a wedding where the couple picks out the flowers? What about the beautiful flowing gowns and dresses that the bride and her bridesmaid's wear, or the smartly trimmed suits and pressed tuxedos that the men in wedding party wear? Have you ever gone to a wedding where the couple to be married has chosen the colors and styles of the clothing to be worn?

The steps involved in planning your funeral are similar to the steps taken for planning a vacation or a wedding. These are events with which we are all familiar.

Let us tell you another story that occurred to someone whom we call Jane. At the age of only fifty-five years, Jane's father passed away unexpectedly after a short illness. Her father had been a successful retailer who loved fishing. Fishing was one of the few things that Jane enjoyed with her father when she was growing up.

For years, Jane's father always told her that someday when he died, he wanted to be cremated and have his ashes scattered over a lake where they often went to fish. Unfortunately, Jane's father never wrote down that *Last Wish* or had never even mentioned it to her mother. After he died and the family was arranging the funeral, Jane told them about her dad's *Last Wish*. At the time, her comments were not well received. There was no one in her family who would believe Jane, including her mother, so she quietly dropped the request.

Jane's family held a lavish funeral service and her father was buried in an expensive metal casket. He was not cremated. Even now, years later, Jane becomes upset thinking that she let her father down because she was not strong enough to convince others in her family of her dad's *Last Wishes*. Of course, we know that this is not true. It was not Jane's fault that her father was not cremated. Her father had failed to inform the rest of his family about his *Last Wishes*. Had he pre-planned his funeral and written down his *Last Wishes*, then his whole family would have had the comfort in knowing that they were following his requests.

It is unfortunate that this type of story is repeated everyday. Yet, with just a little pre-planning you will take control of your funeral ceremony and save family and loved ones from unneeded anguish. Although there is no guarantee that what may be contained on your *Last Wishes* forms will be carried out by your loved ones, you can be certain that if you do not communicate your wishes on the forms, no-one will not know about them.

The previous example clearly shows that in most important moments in your life, planning is important. A person's funeral is a milestone and extremely important for those whom we leave behind. A funeral is the last chance for choices. If you pre-plan your own funeral, you have taken control of that moment of your life and done all that you can to help ease the burdens to your family and friends.

Funerals are an integral part of the grieving process. They furnish structure and support and also assist people through the initial mourning period. Funerals provide a time to honor and remember a life that has been lived. They also provide a time to search for spiritual meaning within the context of each person's religious or philosophical values.

Funerals should not be a matter of impressing but of expressing. To many people the word funeral conjures up images of oppressive organ music, long and solemn religious ceremonies and over-whelming sadness. While such funerals still occur, options for funeral services have changed. People are personalizing services to become a celebration of a life that has been lived. Funerals allow families the opportunity to face their pain while surrounded by people who care about them.

There are as many different types of funerals as there are religions, locales, countries and cultures. With this idea taken into account, this chapter will explain a modern Christian funeral.

FUNERAL CEREMONIES

A funeral ceremony offers many benefits to the survivors of the deceased. It can help to reinforce the reality of the person's death, while it acknowledges and expresses the feelings of loss. A funeral ceremony can offer a spiritual connection with the deceased and help us understand the meaning of life.

A funeral ceremony can be as simple as lighting a few candles and saying a prayer for the deceased. It can also be an elaborate event involving music, readings, and testimonials. Remember your *Last Wishes* for your funeral ceremony should focus on who and what you are.

The three basic versions of a funeral ceremony depend upon when and where the ceremony is held.

- The funeral service is a ceremony in which the deceased person's body is present.
- At a memorial service the deceased's body is not present. Typically a picture or some representation of the deceased is placed in clear view of the attendees.

- A committal service is a ceremony that is held at the graveside immediately before burial or in the case of a cremation, it can be held at the crematory's chapel prior to cremation.

VIEWING OR WAKES

Most people choose a viewing or wake where the deceased's family, friends and acquaintances visit and pay their respects prior to the funeral service, memorial service, or committal service. The viewing is held at a house of worship or a funeral home. Typically the casket holding the deceased can be displayed either open or closed and prayers are offered.

CHURCH FUNERAL CEREMONIES AND GUIDELINES

The majority of funeral services are rituals based upon religious beliefs and customs.. Christians believe that death is not en ending, but a beginning. According to Christian doctrine a loved one who has died has entered eternal life.

If the funeral service is to be held at a church, the clergyman will have a pre-determined order or rite that is to be followed. Most clergy however will allow for unique speakers, music, and readings, as they are able.

The church funeral service may contain all or some of the following:

- **The Procession** - the clergy passes through the congregation to or from the altar,
- **Music** - a hymn or popular music performed by an individual, choir, or the entire congregation,
- **Prayer** - spoken by the clergy, an individual, or the entire congregation,
- **Sermon or Homily** - usually given by the clergy member,
- **Epitaph** - is a brief statement about the life of the deceased individual given by a member of the deceased's family, close friend or the clergy,
- **Scripture** - Bible readings read by family members or friends,
- **Eulogy** - is generally given at the end of the service and it commends the individual who has died. It can be given by the clergy member, family member or close friend (see Chapter V),

- **Poems** - poems can be read by anyone,

- **Flowers** - may be placed in the chapel or where the service is held,

- **Pictures** - memorable pictures of the deceased individual may be placed throughout the room or chapel.

NON-RELIGIOUS FUNERAL CEREMONIES

If you do not wish to have a religious service, you may request a funeral or a memorial service at your home, the funeral home or another available location. The design of the ceremony should reflect your beliefs and feelings and can incorporate as many of the previously mentioned items as you wish. Seek the counsel of the funeral director who can advise you of any local requirements for holding a service in a private setting based upon your personal philosophy.

In this chapter we will provide sample forms and additional information helpful in making your selections. You may note as you proceed with this chapter that the forms are thorough and often ask you to insert information that may be difficult to obtain. Remember that one of the reasons for completing the forms is to assist your survivors. Any information that you provide will be very helpful. The actual forms in the back of the manual are formatted as full pages containing much larger type and multiple entry spaces than the small samples we use in this chapter.

INSTRUCTIONS

General Information

The *General Information* form is used for recording your personal information.

```
General Information
Full Name_____
Nick Name_____
Maiden Name _____
Date of Birth _____
Place of Birth _____
Social Security Number ___-___-___
```

- Full Name: Include your first, middle and last names. Use full names, no initials.

- Nick Name: Include any nicknames or pseudonyms you may have.

- Maiden Name: Include your full maiden name. Use full names, no initials.

- Date of Birth: Include your month, day and year.

- Place of Birth: Include city, state and zip code.

- Social Security Number: Include the number as given to you by the Social Security Administration.

Marital Status

The *Marital Status and Information* form is used to record your marital status and marriage information.

> # Marital Information
> __Married   __Single   __Divorced
> __Widow   __Widower
>
> Current Marriage
> Marriage Date _____   Place _____
>
> Previous Marriages
> Marriage Date _____   Place _____

- Married, Single, Divorced, Widow/Widower: Place an X or checkmark next to the appropriate status.
- Current Marriage: Include the anniversary date and location for your last wedding ceremony.
- Previous Marriages: Include the anniversary date and location for your previous wedding ceremonies.

Religious Information

The *Religious Information* form is used to record your membership of your church. If you are not currently a member of a local church, list your hometown church or a church where you would like to have a funeral service, or leave the information blank.

```
┌─────────────────────────────────────────────┐
│          Religious Information                │
│   Religion_____         │
│   Church Name_____         │
│   Church Address_____         │
│                _____          │
│   Telephone_____         │
│   Priest/Minister_____         │
└─────────────────────────────────────────────┘
```

- Religion: Include the proper name for the religion and denomination.

- Church Name: Include the name of the church.

- Church Address: Include the physical address of the church with the street, city, state and zip code.

- Telephone: Include the church office telephone number with area code.

- Priest/Minister: Include the name of your clergy leader.

Veteran Information

The *Veteran Information* form is used to record information pertaining to your military service. If you need information, contact your local Veterans' Service Office or Veterans' Affairs Office for information on various benefits available. Veterans are eligible for numerous funeral benefits including free military burial, a flag for the burial, burial in a national grave, free headstone and/or a grave marker from the Veterans' Affairs Department. To contact the Veterans' Affairs Department see the appendix for the proper address and phone number.

If you qualify for a military funeral, the ceremony may include a band, military escorts, caisson and colors. A military person in charge of arranging the details will inform the clergy and family of the instructions as outlined by various branches of the armed forces.

The military benefit may also include the presence of military casket bearers, a firing squad, and the playing of taps at the graveside. The rest of the ceremony is the same as any regular service. In the case of military veterans, the national flag is often draped as a pall over the casket symbolizing the deceased's service in the military.

Veteran Information

Service / Branch _____

Date and Place of Enlistment _____

Date of Discharge _____

Rank and Service Number _____

Veterans' Administration Claim # _____

War / Conflicts / Tours of Duty _____

Commendations Received _____

- Service/Branch: Include the service name and branch for which you served.

- Date and Place of Enlistment: Include the date you enlisted or reported for duty and the city and state where you reported.

- Date of Discharge: Include the date of your discharge.

- Rank and Service Number: Include the final rank at discharge and your service number.

- Veterans' Administration Claim #: If you have been in contact with the Veteran Affairs Department, include your claim number.

- War/Conflicts/Tours of Duty: Include any wars, conflicts and locations of tours of duty during your tenure in the service.

- Commendation Received: Include any distinguishing honors or medals you received.

Immediate Family

The *Immediate Family* form is used to record information about your immediate family. You may have this information documented in an address book or similar location, but the names of your family will not necessarily be listed as such. The inclusion of this form provides a quick reference that will be helpful in writing your obituary and in contacting family at the time of death.

Immediate Family
For use in Notification and Obituary
Relationship/Name/Date of Birth/City/State/Telephone
Spouse_____
Parent_____
Parent_____
Child_____
Child_____
Grand-child_____
Grand-child_____
Sibling_____
Other_____
Other_____

- Spouse: Include the name of your current spouse, if applicable, using full first, middle and last name.

- Parent: Include the names of your parents, using first, middle and last names.

- Child: Include the names of your children, using first, middle and last names.

- Grandchild: Include the names of your grand children, using first, middle and last names.

- Siblings: Include the names of your brothers and/or sisters, using first, middle and last names.

- Other: Include the names of other family member, using first, middle and last names.

Membership in Professional, Union, and Fraternal Organizations

The *Membership in Professional, Union and Fraternal Organization* form is used to record information about your various memberships and affiliations. Many organizations offer different services to members for their funerals. Check with your organizations and learn what they offer. This form will be helpful in writing your obituary and in notifying the organizations upon your death.

Membership in Professional, Union, And Fraternal Organizations

For use in Notification and Obituary

Name   Address   Telephone   Dates
_____

- Name/Address/Telephone/Dates: Include the full name, address (including the city, state and zip code), area code, telephone number and the dates of your membership in each separate organization.

Community and Voluntary Services

The *Community and Voluntary Services* form is used to record information about your various voluntary and community organizations in which you were or are a member. This form will be helpful in writing your obituary and in notifying the organizations upon your death.

```
┌─────────────────────────────────────────────┐
│                                             │
│     Community and Voluntary                 │
│              Services                       │
│     For use in Notification and Obituary    │
│                                             │
│       Name/Address/Telephone/Dates          │
│     _____          │
│                                             │
└─────────────────────────────────────────────┘
```

- Name/Address/Telephone/Dates: Include the full name, address (including the city, state and zip code), area code, phone number and the dates of your membership in each separate organization.

Education

The *Education* form is used to record information about the schools and institutions of higher learning that you have attended. This form will be helpful in writing your obituary and in notifying these institutions upon your death.

Education
For use in Obituary
Type   Name/City/State/Degree/Dates Attended
High School_____
Trade School_____
College_____
Graduate College_____
Certificates_____

- High School: Include the full name, address (including the city, state and zip code), the diploma attained, honors conferred, and the dates you attended.

- Trade School: Include the full name, address (including the city, state and zip code), the type of degree attained, honors conferred, and the dates you attended.

- College: Include the full name, address (including the city, state and zip code), the type of degree attained, honors conferred, and the dates you attended.

- Graduate School: Include the full name, address (including the city, state and zip code), the type of degree attained, honors conferred, and the dates you attended.

- Certificates: Include the full name, address (including the city, state and zip code), the type of certificates attained, honors conferred, and the dates you attended.

Employers

The *Employers* form is used to record your current and as many former employers as you wish in the spaces provided. This form will be helpful in writing your obituary.

Employers
For use in Obituary
Company/Occupation/Location/Dates

_____

- Company: Include the full name of the company where you are employed or have worked.

- Occupation: Include your title and or occupation for each company.

- Location: Include the full address with the city, state and zip code of each company.

- Dates: Include the dates that each company employed you.

Friends/Employers/Colleagues

The *Friends/Employers/Colleagues* form is used to record information about your friends, employers and co-workers. This form will be useful to contact the individuals upon your death, since these individuals may not hear about your death any other way.

Friends/Employers/Colleagues
For use in Death Notification

Tele-
Relationship/Name/Date of Birth/City/State/Phone
Friend_____
Employer_____
Colleagues_____

- Friend: Include full name, address (including the city, state and zip code), and telephone number including area code.

- Employer: Include full name, address (including the city, state and zip code), and telephone number including area code.

- Colleagues: Include full names, address (including the city, state and zip code), and telephone number including area code.

Attorney Information

The *Attorney Information* form is used to record the information about your attorney. Enter the appropriate information in the space provided.

Attorney Information
Firm Name_____

Attorney Name_____

Address_____

City / State_____

Telephone_____

- Firm Name: If applicable, include the name of the law firm that you have retained.

- Attorney Name: Include the name of the Attorney that represents you.

- Address: Include the number and street of your attorney.

- City/State: Include the city, state and zip code of your attorney.

- Telephone: Include your attorney's telephone number.

Executor Information

The *Executor Information* form is used to record the information about your appointed Executor. An executor is a person named in your Will who is responsible for ensuring that the provisions in your Will are completed. This person may be any competent adult, bank or trust company. Many people choose their spouse, attorney or a close relative.

Executor Information
Name_____
Address_____
City / State_____
Telephone_____

- Name/Address/City/State/Telephone: Include full name, street address, the city, state and zip code, and telephone number including area code.

Documents

The *Documents* form is used to record information regarding all important papers and documents that you have gathered throughout the years.

- **Will:** A will is a legal document that specifies how your property and obligations will be handled upon your death. In a will you can honor the important people in your life with a substantial gift or a sentimental token. You can also direct donations to charitable organizations to continue their good work after your death.

    A will may include provisions for trusts and usually names an executor or individual that will oversee the distribution of assets. It may also list contingencies such as, who will act as executor if the named executor is unable to fulfill that obligation.

    If you do not have a will, or other estate planning documents, your property may not be distributed the way you wish. Your property will be distributed according to the laws of the state where you live. If you have a will you may want to review it to ensure that your present circumstances are reflected.

- **Health Care Directives:** The health care directive, also known as an advance directive, is a document created to dictate your care when you are no longer able to make decisions for yourself. An advance directive can help save money for the estate and help to reduce the emotional trauma of a prolonged terminal condition. In the absence of an advance directive, physicians and family may be motivated to try every available procedure, surgery, or device to prolong life.

There are two main documents that are used by individuals to provide advance directives; these are a living will and a health care power of attorney.

- **Living Will:** A living will is a document in which you state what life sustaining procedures should be withheld or withdrawn if you become terminally ill, or permanently unconscious and are unable to make those decisions.

- **Health Care Power of Attorney:** A health care power of attorney is a document which appoints and authorizes an agent to make health care decisions in the event you are unable to make medical decisions.

A living will is similar to, but different from a health care power of attorney. With a health care power of attorney, one is appointed to act on your behalf if you are unable to do so. A living will is a personal, individual declaration of your choices and instructions.

Copies of your living will and or health care power of attorney should be provided to your physicians, attorney, executor and immediate family. The original documents should be stored in a place where they can be easily retrieved as necessary.

- **Living Trust:** A living trust is a formal arrangement established by you to transfer your assets to another person or persons. The purpose of a living trust is to avoid many of the costs and problems associated with the probate process upon your death or incapacity.

- **Power of Attorney:** A power of attorney is a legal document that grants authority to someone to handle decisions other than health care matters. You may want this document if you are unable to handle personal matters for some period of time, due to an extended illness or vacation. Once appointed, the attorney may have the authority to deal with your financial accounts, property, real estate, and other matters.

Documents

Document	Do You Have? Y / N	Other Location/Account#/Notes
Will	__ __	_____
Living Will	__ __	_____
Living Trust	__ __	_____
Medical Power of Attorney	__ __	_____
Cemetery Plot Deed	__ __	_____
Safe Deposit Box	__ __	_____
Safe Deposit Box Key	__ __	_____
Automobile Titles	__ __	_____
Birth Certificate	__ __	_____
Passport	__ __	_____
Income Tax Records	__ __	_____
Life Insurance	__ __	_____
Savings Account	__ __	_____
Checking Account	__ __	_____
Mortgage Papers/Deeds	__ __	_____
Other Documents		_____

- Will: Place a check mark beneath 'yes' or 'no' and the location where the document is located. List the account number or reference number of the document and any other notes that may be pertinent.

- Living Will: Place a check mark beneath 'yes' or 'no' and the location where the document can be found. List the account number or reference number of the document and any other notes that may be pertinent.

- Living Trust: Place a check mark beneath 'yes' or 'no' and the location where the document can be found. List the account number or reference number of the document and any other notes that may be pertinent.

- Medical Power of Attorney: Place a check mark beneath 'yes' or 'no' and the location where the document can be found. List the account number or reference number of the document and any other notes that may be pertinent.

- Cemetery Plot Deed: Place a check mark beneath 'yes' or 'no' and the location where the document can be found. List the account number or reference number of the document and any other notes that may be pertinent.

- Safe Deposit Box: Place a check mark beneath 'yes' or 'no' and the bank name and address where the box can be found. List the account number or reference number of the document and any other notes that may be pertinent.

- Safe Deposit Box Key: Place a check mark beneath 'yes' or 'no' and the location where the key can be found. List the account number or reference number of the box and any other notes that may be pertinent.

- Automobile Titles: Place a check mark beneath 'yes' or 'no' and the location where the certificate can be found. List the account number or reference number of the document and any other notes that may be pertinent.

- Birth Certificate: Place a check mark beneath 'yes' or 'no' and the location where the certificate can be found.

- Passport: Place a check mark beneath 'yes' or 'no' and the location where your passport can be found.

- Income Tax Records: Place a check mark beneath 'yes' or 'no' and the location where the document can be found.

- Life Insurance: Place a check mark beneath 'yes' or 'no' and the location where the document can be found. List the account number or reference number of the document and any other notes that may be pertinent.

- Savings Account: Place a check mark beneath 'yes' or 'no' and the location where the document can be found. List the account number or reference number of the document and any other notes that may be pertinent.

- Checking Account: Place a check mark beneath 'yes' or 'no' and the location where the document can be found. List the account number or reference number of the document and any other notes that may be pertinent.

- Mortgage Papers/Deeds: Place a check mark beneath 'yes' or 'no' and the location where the document can be found. List the account number or reference number of the document and any other notes that may be pertinent.

- Other Documents: Identify the other document and place a check mark beneath 'yes' or 'no' and the location where the documents can be found. List the account number or reference number of the document and any other notes that may be pertinent.

Newspapers or Publications

The *Newspapers or Publications* form is used to list those publications where your obituary notice should be printed. An obituary is a notice of a death, which is published in a newspaper or similar publication. It usually contains a brief biography of the deceased and includes personal statistics and family information. Some newspapers use a standard format for obituaries and provide a form which, when completed, contains all the necessary information. An obituary may also be used to announce the date and time of a memorial service.

If a memorial fund is to be established it is important to determine this early enough so that the announcement can be made in the obituary. The public is directed where to send their donations to the custodian of the fund until it is sent to the recipient. Care should be taken that the words "in lieu of flowers" are never used because it may confuse well-meaning people from making any donations at all.

Over the years it has become quite common for people to write their own obituary. If you know exactly what you want written, include it in the space provided on the forms. If you are unsure what to include in your obituary, write some key points you would like to see written in your obituary and your family will see that it gets put into the proper form.

Newspapers or Publications

For Obituary Notice

Name   Address   Telephone

_____

- Name/Address/Telephone: Include the newspapers full name, address (including the city, state and zip code), and the telephone number, including area code.

Disposition of Remains

The *Disposition of Remains* form is used to record your wishes for the final disposition of your remains. The Christian concept holds that the body, during the earthly life is a temple of God's Spirit. So, regardless of the method of disposal, the body after death is to be treated with reverence and dignity. You will find additional information about disposition options bellow.

```
        Final Disposition of
              Remains
     Type              Yes  No
   Body Donation
   for Research        _____
   Cremation           _____
   Burial              _____
```

- Body Donation for Research: Place an 'X' or a check mark beneath the appropriate 'yes' or 'no' column.
- Cremation: List the type of cremation and place an 'X' or check mark beneath the appropriate 'yes' or 'no' column.
- Burial: List the type of burial and place an 'X' or check mark beneath the appropriate 'yes' or 'no' column.

Medical School / Science

The *Medical School/Science* form is used to record information about where and how you would like to donate your body to a medical school or to science.

Death provides many of us with a chance to make a valuable gift to humanity. Most religions approve of body and organ donation for medical and dental teaching, research, and transplants.

- **Medical Research:** If you plan to donate your body to medical research after death, it is recommended that you contact the institution for which your gift is intended. In some urban areas, teaching medical schools may have an ample supply of body donations, and may not be able to accept your gift. When you arrange for your gift, specify whether or not the institution may donate your body to another school. It is important to inquire about the specific arrangements to be used at the time of death in order to avoid additional costs. After medical study, the body is usually cremated, with burial or scattering of ashes in a university plot. Often the cremains or remains may be returned to the family for burial within a year or two. This option should be made known at the time of donation.

- **Organ Donation:** With advances in medical science organ transplants have become fairly common. Donation at a time of death is a gift of life. In addition to heart, liver, lungs and pancreas, other organs, tissues, corneas, and bones may also be donated. Organs are in short supply, because they can be donated only under certain conditions. Circumstances surrounding death may limit this option. If you wish to aid the living with an organ donation, be certain that your next-of-kin and your physician know your preference. This is important for your family to understand your wishes, since even when a person has signed an organ donor's card, doctors usually will not remove the organs if the family objects. In addition to family notification, your intent to donate organs should be noted on any medical or hospital record, and driver's license. Those individuals who choose to donate organs can still have an open-casket viewing or funeral. Life is a precious gift and you may have comfort in knowing that another's life can be saved.

To summarize if you elect to donate vital organs upon your death always:

- carry organ donor cards,

- sign the donor space on the back of your license,

- include your decision in your Last Will & Testament, and

- inform your friends and loved ones of your *Last Wishes*.

It is important to honor the wishes of those who want to donate all or part of their bodies upon death. Once the individual choice is made, the funeral home is required to abide by your wishes. For more information on organ donation, please refer to the appendix at the back of this manual.

Medical School / Science

Name of School/Organization/Address

Type of Donation

_____ Corpse

_____ Organs

_____ Other Organs

- Corpse/Organs/Other Organs: Include the recipient school or organization's full name, address (including the city, state and zip code), and the type of donation that you have decided to make.

Cremation

The *Cremation* form is used to record the information necessary for cremation.

Cremation is the heating process that incinerates human remains. The body is contained in a rigid container and is placed in a specialized furnace or retort. The cremation process exposes the body to an open flame, intense heat and evaporation, reducing the bone fragments in two or three hours. Although cremated remains do have the appearance of ashes; they consist primarily of bone fragments. Depending upon the size of the body, cremation results in three to nine pounds of remains.

The process of cremation may be selected due to religious beliefs, ethnic customs or costs. Most states require a two-day waiting period between the time of death and the cremation. The waiting period provides the necessary time for the funeral director to file for required permits and to receive proper authorizations.

One advantage of cremation is that it is generally less expensive than a burial. A cremation ceremony also allows you to be more creative in directing the disposal of your ashes. The cremains may be stored for burial or scattered as desired. A possible disadvantage of cremation happens when a family chooses not to have any type of memorial service. This may leave family and friends confused about the mourning process and does not enable them to feel closure.

In addition to cremation, there are other choices to consider, a visitation, funeral ceremony and/or memorial services are among them. Some states allow funeral homes to rent caskets, therefore a viewing of the deceased can be held before cremation. Additionally the cremation may take place first, followed by the memorial service. Depending upon the final resting-place, cremated remains are placed in a temporary container for transport to the burial site. For a more permanent container, the remains can be maintained in an urn, columbarium, scattered in a special place, or buried. Laws governing the disposal of cremated remains vary from state to state. You should check the legal and procedural requirements with your funeral director, crematory or cemetery.

The customer's designation of intentions is a specific form that the funeral director will complete if you select cremation. It includes a space for "disposal of cremated remains". Final resting places for your cremated remains can be as follows: a cemetery burial, in an urn which is a sealing container that conveniently holds the cremains of a body, and in a columbarium which is a vault with spaces designed for storing urns. One can also opt for the widely known scattering of ashes.

Cremation

Category	Name/Address/Location
Preferred Crematory	_____
Designation of Intentions	_____
Final Resting Place of Remains	Urn_____
	Columbarium_____
	Buried_____
	Scattered_____

- Preferred Crematory: Include full name and the address including the city, state and zip code here.
- Designation of Intentions: If applicable, include the location of this document here.
- Final Resting Place of Remains: Record your *Last Wishes* here.

Burial / Cemetery or Gravesite

The *Burial / Cemetery or Gravesite* form is used to record information about the site of the final resting-place of the deceased body.

Traditional burial in the ground is at present the preference of most people, but the option of cremation is increasing. In traditional burials you select a vault and casket, purchase a cemetery plot or memorial park plot, and plan a service according to your *Last Wishes*.

The advantages of a burial ceremony may include religious or family tradition you wish to follow. With a burial, there is a place for your survivors to return to whenever they wish to be comforted or just pay their respects over time. Many people feel that a burial just feels more personal. A disadvantage of burial is related to the cemetery and the expense involved with the continued maintenance of a gravesite and the land fees associated with the land used.

At a memorial park you purchase a plot, but your memory is retained with a memorial or marker, while your remains are placed somewhere else.

Additional information pertaining to burial is below:

- Grave Liners: Grave liners are usually cement slabs that the casket is placed upon burial. Grave liners are not legally required but are mandated by many cemeteries to protect the ground from settling.

- Vault: A vault is an outer burial container that the casket fits into. Vaults are not legally required but may be required by many cemeteries to protect the ground from settling.

- Cemetery Deed: A cemetery deed is the document from the cemetery that establishes your right to bury the deceased in the plot.

- Entombment: Entombment is a burial in an aboveground crypt in a mausoleum or in a lawn crypt.

- Outer Interment Receptacle: Outer interment receptacle is a container in the ground, in which the casket is placed. Vaults and grave liners are some examples. Some cemeteries require outer interment receptacles to prevent collapse or sinking of the grave.

Burial
Cemetery or Gravesite

Category	Do You Have Yes / No	Name/Address/Location
Cemetery	__ __	_____
Memorial Park	__ __	_____
Grave Site Purchased	__ __	_____
Grave Deed	__ __	_____
Grave or Niche	__ __	_____
Grave Liner Preference		_____
Entombment	__ __	_____
Crypt	__ __	_____

- Preferred Burial - Cemetery /Memorial Park: Place a check mark beneath 'yes' or 'no' and include the location where the cemetery or park can be found.

- Grave Site Purchased: Place a check mark beneath 'yes' or 'no' and include the location where the gravesite can be found. List the account number or reference number of the document and any other notes that may be pertinent.

- Grave Deed: Place a check mark beneath 'yes' or 'no' and include the location where the documents can be found. List the account number or reference number of the document and any other notes that may be pertinent.

- Grave or Niche: Place a check mark beneath 'yes' or 'no' and include the location where the grave or niche can be found.

- Grave Liner Preference: Place a check mark beneath 'yes' or 'no' and a description of the grave liner that you prefer.

- Entombment: Place a check mark beneath 'yes' or 'no' and a description of the tomb that you prefer.

- Crypt: Place a check mark beneath 'yes' or 'no' and include a description of the crypt that you prefer.

Burial Instructions – Clothing and Other Articles

The *Burial Instructions* form is used to record any information regarding specific clothing and other items intended for the burial or an open casket funeral service. This form will suggest detailed instructions for survivors to follow upon your death.

The old adage, "You can't take it with you" may not be true. Although, you can't be buried in your house, a recent news item featured a person who had been buried inside his Cadillac! Your *Last Wishes* will help your survivors to make correct decisions when you are buried.

Burial Instructions Clothing or Other Articles		
Items	**Request Yes / No**	**Description**
Recommended Special Burial Clothing	__ __	_____
Recommended Every Day Clothing	__ __	_____
Other Burial Items	__ __	_____

- Recommended Special Burial Clothing: Place a check mark beneath 'yes' or 'no' and a detailed location and description of any special articles of clothing for burial or cremation.

- Recommended Every Day Clothing: Place a check mark beneath 'yes' or 'no' and a detailed location and description of any everyday articles of clothing for burial or cremation.

- Other Burial Items: Place a check mark beneath the 'yes' or 'no' and list any additional items to be placed in the casket for burial here. For example you might list a favorite book, photograph, golf club, tennis racket, flag or flowers, etc. Designate the location of any item that may be difficult to find.

Burial Instructions – Funeral Home Wishes

The *Burial Instructions Funeral Home Wishes* form is used to record information about the funeral home that you have selected. The form will be of tremendous help to the funeral director and your family.

Pre-arrangement allows for unhurried decisions about the professional services that may be required at the time of a person's funeral. Even if you are young, it is still wise to make your *Last Wishes* known should an untimely death befall you. If you are retired or in poor health, make the time to complete your *Last Wishes* and meet with a funeral director.

Funeral pre-arrangement is part of sensible estate planning. During discussions with a funeral director, you are given opportunities to ask questions. This is a time to fully understand the services performed and the costs involved.

There are several ways to pre-fund funeral expenses. Pre-funding offers the advantage of paying for a funeral when you can afford it, and it helps prevent possible financial and emotional burdens to loved ones. Most states have legislation related to prepaid funerals, requirements for how monies can be set aside, conditions for cancellation, and regulations concerning who can sell prepaid funerals. When deciding to purchase a prepaid plan, look for one that has a revocable, guaranteed price that guarantees the funeral you desire regardless of future price increases, and allows for a partial or full refund if you change your plans. Be sure you understand the details of payment whether in one lump sum or installment payments.

As mentioned in *Chapter IV, Funeral Practices*, there are different types of funeral services from which to choose. They include:

- a funeral service with the body present,
- a memorial service without the body present and not requiring extensive services or the expense of a mortician, and
- a committal at the graveside immediately before burial or in a crematory chapel before cremation.

The staff of a funeral home will carry out the plans for preparation of the body, burial decisions, memorial services, and administers the details of a funeral.

The first step in pre-planning a funeral is to select a funeral home and associated funeral director with which you will feel comfortable. Once the funeral home is selected, a meeting, which is referred to as the arrangement conference can be scheduled. This is generally done at the funeral home, but it may also take place in your home or over the telephone.

When meeting the funeral director, you will be given a price list listing detailed costs associated with each item available. The price list should include, but not be limited to caskets, burial expenses, funeral services and all other services the funeral home has available. After you have made your selections, you will be given an itemized statement, which usually will include contractual language. Do not sign any papers that will legally obligate you to pay for the cost of the funeral unless you have made your final choice. Shop around, visit other funeral homes and compare services and prices before you finalize your purchase. If you make the arrangements by telephone, you will be given the price list when you receive an itemized statement. Additional pricing information is discussed later in this chapter. See the Appendix for more information on consumer rights.

It is important to keep in mind that part of the decision making process for pre-planning your funeral should include your estate's financial ability to pay. Without the resources to pay for the funeral in advance, many funeral homes may allow the purchase to be financed after a small down payment. Be sure to discuss this matter with the funeral director.

Many funeral homes will offer a discount if you pre-purchase service arrangements with them. Pre-payment can lift much of the financial burden from survivors, while allowing you to select the type of funeral arrangements you want. Pre-need plans are regulated by the Funeral Rule If you desire to pre-pay, keep in mind that if you are buried in a different place, or later change your intentions, the funeral home where you pre-purchased may keep a percentage of the pre-payment already given to them. Make certain that the language about refunds is spelled out in plain English on the itemized statement.

Since you are paying for the arrangements, keep in mind that you are the customer; as the customer, you have certain rights. Although the rights you have as a consumer differ from state to state, it is always important to shop around at different funeral homes. Feel free to ask as many questions as you can about the arrangements you intend to make.

Anyone in the family can make the funeral arrangements for the deceased. When pre-planning, designate the person that is the main point of contact for the funeral director after your death. This is the ideal time to discuss and agree with other family members about the type of services and what is to be purchased. Remember this person becomes the customer and that person will ultimately be responsible for the bill unless it is prepaid.

In most states, a person can not be buried without the aid of a licensed and registered mortician, who is usually the funeral director. Only a funeral director may make funeral arrangements concerning the care, moving, preparation and burial or cremation of the deceased. At the very least, the funeral director will file the death certificate, transfer the body, coordinate with cemetery or crematory representatives, make the necessary preparations, and move the body to the cemetery or crematory.

In many states, a casket is not necessary for burial, but most cemeteries require the use of a suitable container. The container can be an ornately covered casket made from fine bronze, aluminum, veneer wood and can be an unfinished wooden box or a form of alternative container. These can be constructed of pressed wood, cardboard, composition materials, canvas or other materials.

Be aware that many cemeteries require burial vaults or grave liners to prevent the collapse or sinking of the grave. The vaults and liners can add considerable cost to the expense of a funeral. If you do not want to buy a burial vault, be sure to choose a cemetery where one is not required.

A cemetery may require the embalming of the deceased. If there is an open casket at the viewing, then embalming is required. A funeral home can not refuse to embalm a body or even handle a body, regardless of the cause of death. This includes the bodies of persons who have died of an infectious disease such as AIDS, hepatitis, malaria or any other infectious disease. The fees associated with embalming should be clearly stated on both the funeral homes' price list and on the itemized statement of services.

You may wonder at this point just what the final costs will be. Of course, the costs can vary greatly, depending on the funeral home and on the type of services that you choose. For example, if the service you select involves viewing the remains, the funeral home will require embalming and preparation of the body, which can be expensive. There is also a tremendous range in the price of caskets, depending on which style, the type of wood, the lining, and the amount of decoration on the outside.

There are several steps and choices involved in the process of the funeral arrangements all of which determine the final cost associated with your *Last Wishes*. Most states do not regulate the prices charged by funeral homes; what is regulated is that they must clearly list their prices and follow strict guidelines in their business practices. The least expensive type of funeral service is direct burial or direct cremation without any other services required of the funeral home.

For your information, the Funeral Rule states that funeral homes and funeral directors **may not** do the following:

- pressure their customer to select certain services or merchandise,
- charge additional fees for filing the death certificate or getting it medically certified,
- charge a handling fee for paying third parties on your behalf,
- charge a fee for handling a casket provided by the customer,
- charge for any service or merchandise not selected by the customer previously,
- charge interest on an outstanding balance unless this charge is disclosed at the time the funeral arrangements were initially made and are stated in the itemized statement,
- no person other than the licensed funeral director can prepare the body, or supervise the burial,
- misrepresent laws and regulations relating to funeral directing, and
- change your arrangements without prior approval.

Remember that you do not have to accept services or merchandise you don't want! Be informed of all charges in advance! Always get a receipt when you making a payment! While you are pre-arranging with the funeral home, please keep in mind the executor will need more than one copy of the death certificate. Certified copies of the death certificate are needed for insurance companies, banks, and certain creditors. The funeral director can only charge you the actual fee for the death certificate. Death certificates are filed by the funeral director with the Registrar of Vital Records in the locality where the death occurred.

There are also different processes that can be used to address the deceased person's body in preparation for funeral and burial. The embalming process disinfects, preserves and restores the body to an acceptable physical. The embalming process begins with the thorough washing and disinfecting of the body. Embalming chemicals are injected into the body through one of the arteries. Embalming is solely for short-term preservation of the body; its purpose is to delay decomposition. This provides necessary time to complete arrangements and services, which may take several days to accomplish and to transport the body to another location, if necessary.

Embalming is not required by law, nor is it a routine process. If you have not pre-arranged, funeral directors are required to ask permission of the deceased's next-of-kin verbally or in writing before embalming. A licensed professional, such as the funeral director or a licensed embalmer must perform this service. The cost for embalming is extra. A few states do require embalming if the body is to be transported by common carrier or if a communicable or contagious disease caused death.

Another service that most funeral homes provide is the topical disinfecting. A topical disinfecting is the external cleaning of the body by the funeral director or their assistant. There is always a fee for this process.

Other fees that you can expect to be charged for and you must decide upon are:

- **Transfer of Remains Fee**: The transfer of remains fee is charged when a body has to be moved from the place where death occurs to the funeral home,

- **Custodial Fee**: The custodial fee may be charged for the number of days the deceased person's body is held. It is often charged when the funeral home does nothing else,

- **Refrigeration Fee**: The refrigeration fee is charged by some funeral homes for cooling the body when embalming is not selected.

If you are involved in the arrangements of your funeral or that of a loved one's funeral and you become upset with services rendered, there are places that you can turn to. Each state has a Bureau of Funeral Directing, or equivalent department, that deals with such issues. Check with your state's Department of Health for further information. There also are numerous funeral home organizations listed in the Appendix at the back of this manual for you to contact if the funeral home that you have used is a member.

Burial Instructions
Funeral Home Wishes

Items	Request Yes/No	Instructions
Designated Contact		_____
Pre-Plan With Funeral Home?	__ __	_____
Recommended Funeral Home	__ __	_____
Recommended Funeral Director	__ __	_____

- Designated Contact: List the name of the designated contact.

- Pre-Plan With A Funeral Home: Place a checkmark beneath 'yes' or 'no' and list your instructions.

- Recommended Funeral Home: Place a checkmark beneath 'yes' or 'no' and list your instructions.

- Recommended Funeral Director: Place a checkmark beneath 'yes' or 'no' and list your instructions.

Casket Information

The *Casket Information* form is used to record the information about your preferences for a casket.

There are many different choices for all the various styles and types of casket construction that it is virtually unlimited, but keep in mind that the costs can also be unlimited, too.

The casket is the container in which the deceased is placed for the funeral service, for viewing, and for burial. Caskets vary widely in style and price and typically are sold for their visual appeal and they generally are made of metal or wood, although some are constructed of fiberglass or plastic. Most metal caskets are made from rolled steel in different gauges – the lower the gauge, the thicker the steel. Wooden caskets come in hardwood, softwood or plywood. Some caskets may have religious symbols in the head panel or other hardware that may be appealing.

The terms "gasket", "protective" and "sealer" are frequently used to describe a metal casket. These terms mean that the casket has a rubber gasket or other features that delay the penetration of water and prevent rust. Some metal caskets come with a warranty for longevity. The protective features in caskets add to their cost.

Unlike metal caskets, wooden caskets generally do not have a gasket and do not carry a warranty for longevity. However, manufacturers of both wooden and metal caskets usually warrant workmanship and materials.

As you can see, when selecting a casket there are many factors to consider other than simply color or eye appeal. Take time to choose a casket that is right for you.

Under the Funeral Rule, funeral providers are prohibited from making claims that caskets or vaults will repel water and resist dirt and other gravesite substances when that is not true.

Remember that if a gasket is chosen, other items may need to be purchased regarding choice of entombment. Also, some cemeteries require outer internment receptacles to prevent collapse or sinking of the grave. These include grave liner, vault, entombment, and outer internment receptacles described elsewhere in this chapter.

Casket Information

Items	Request Yes/No	Description
Casket Purchased	__ __	_____
Casket Preferences		
Metal	__ __	_____
Hardwood	__ __	_____
Pine Box	__ __	_____
Fabric Cover	__ __	_____
Environmental	__ __	_____
Other Style	__ __	_____
Other Preferences	_____	

- Casket Purchased: Place a check mark beneath 'yes' or ' no' and the name of the funeral home.

- Casket Preferences: metal/hardwood/pine box/fabric over/environmental/other style: Place a check mark beneath 'yes' or 'no' and the description and style of the casket that you prefer.

- Other Preferences: Include any other information of casket preferences.

Gravestones and Monuments

The *Gravestone and Monuments* form is used to record the information for your gravestone. This form will be helpful to your survivors upon your death.

Many cemeteries still allow families to choose their gravestone although there may be requirements as to height or size depending on the site. Memorial parks require the stones to be flat and level with the ground. The cemetery or memorial park that you choose may be owned by your church, the town you live in or by a private company.

Most states regulate cemeteries or crematories. If you have a complaint it is advisable to notify the Department of the State Division of Cemeteries. However, if the cemetery is owned by a religious organization or is municipally owned, it may not be subject to regulation.

Whether it is known as a gravestone, headstone or monument, the proliferation of grave markers has been with us for hundreds of years. A gravestone should have a name, date of birth, date of death, may indicate names of closest relatives, and it may have an inscription that is known as an epitaph. Considered as the deceased's last opportunity to make a statement, an epitaph can make a bold, final proclamation or it may be a riddle for future generations to ponder. Although a relative may label your gravestone, it can be self-written. There are numerous books written about the epitaphs found on gravestones. Although we do not go into it at any length it is another way to have the last word and it should be included among your *Last Wishes*.

Gravestones and Monuments

Category	Do You Have Yes / No	Description
Headstone	__ __	_____
Material Of Monument		_____
General Shape Of Monument		_____
General Size Of Monument		_____
Other Monument Preferences		_____
Self-Written Epitaph	__ __	_____

- Headstone: Place a checkmark beneath 'yes' or 'no' with a description of the headstone you would like.

- Material of Monument: Include the information on the material that for the monument.

- General Shape of Monument: Include the information about the shape of monument that you would like.

- General Size of Monument: Include the information about the size of monument that you would like.

- Other Monument Preference: Include the any other information about the monument that you would like.

- Self-Written Epitaph: Place a checkmark beneath 'yes' or 'no' with a description of the epitaph (or inscription) you would like.

Funeral Ceremony Preferences

The *Funeral Ceremony Preferences* form records your wishes about ceremony preferences and is very helpful to your survivors.

Funerals are an integral part of the grieving process. They provide structure and support to assist people through the initial mourning period. They provide a time to honor and remember a life that has ended. Funerals help to "search for meaning" within the context of each person's religious or philosophical values.

A viewing and funerals help confirm the reality of death to the person's loved ones, which is an important step in the healing process. A funeral brings together a community of mourners so that they can share their emotions and support each other during a difficult time.

Funerals need not be a matter of impressing but of expressing. To many people the word funeral conjures up certain images. Funeral services are changing. Families are personalizing services to become a celebration of a life. Funerals allow the opportunity for loved ones to face their pain while surrounded by people who care about them.

Some of the additional choices for pre-planning your funeral may include the following:

- **Memorial Gifts**: Choose a charity or institution that can be a recipient of memorial gifts in your honor. The selected recipient should be one that is of special interest to you or has the characteristic concerns and interest that you share.

- **In Lieu of Flowers Donation**: In recent years, many families who have lost their loved ones may prefer for people to donate the money that they would have spent on flowers to a charitable organization such as The American Cancer Society or Mother Against Drunk Driving. This is a wonderful and generous idea; if you would like this done at the time of your death, name the charitable organization where the contributions may be sent.

- **Favorite Flowers**: Flowers can help express the love and sympathy of friends and, in a limited amount, can add to the beauty of the service. If you have always been a lover of flowers then you are in luck when it comes to the type of flowers for your funeral. On the other hand, many people like flowers but they are not very familiar with the proper names or have no idea what they would prefer. You can suggest a type of flower that you would like at your funeral. Since selected flowers may be out of season and very costly to obtain, list alternative choices. A church may limit the number of flower arrangements that may be included for a funeral. The church may also limit the flowers intended for the altar or the coffin.

In the Appendix many of the standard flowers used for funerals are listed. Make your choice then enter the appropriate information in the space provided.

Funeral Ceremony Preferences

Type of Preference	Request Yes/No	Description Name/Location
Open Casket	__ __	_____
Closed Casket	__ __	_____
Public	__ __	_____
Private	__ __	_____
In Church	__ __	_____
In Funeral Home	__ __	_____
Other Location	__ __	_____
Memorial Gifts	__ __	_____
In Lieu of Flowers	__ __	_____
Favorite Flowers		_____

- Type of Preference - Open or Closed Casket: Place a check mark beneath 'yes' or 'no' and a brief description of what type of ceremony you would like held in your memory. Also include the name and location including city and state of the location you would prefer.

- Type of Preference - Public/Private/In Church/Funeral Home/Other Location: Place a check mark beneath 'yes' or 'no' and a brief description of where you would like a ceremony held in your memory. Also include the name and location including city and state of the location you would prefer.

- Memorial Gifts: Place a checkmark beneath 'yes' or 'no' and the location including city and state where you would like the donations sent.

- In Lieu of Flowers: Place a checkmark beneath 'yes' or 'no' and the location including city and state where you would like the donations sent.

- Favorite Flowers: Include any information on the type and quantity of flowers you would like purchased for your funeral.

Funeral Participants – Part 1

The *Funeral Participants – Part 1* form is used to record whom you would like to preside over your funeral and carry your casket.

If you have selected a funeral service, then you may wish to have some of your friends or family participate directly in the service. People you choose may act as your casket bearers, speakers, music soloists and ushers. Bear in mind that those whom you request will be grieving for your death and it may be difficult for them to fulfill your wishes, but do not fail to list their names in your *Last Wishes*.

- **Casket/Pallbearers**: Casket bearers, also known as pallbearers, are individuals who you select to carry the coffin or casket from the funeral service to the hearse. Persons selected to be pallbearers need to be physically capable of helping to lift the weight of the coffin. Six pallbearers are usually chosen, although up to eight may be used. Women may be pallbearers or a mixture of men and women may be chosen. Sometimes people select three or four husband and wife couples to act as the casket bearers. Honorary pallbearers are persons to whom you offer your respectful appreciation by recognizing them as honorary pallbearers. This distinction may be granted to special people who are physically unable to be active pallbearers.

```
┌─────────────────────────────────────────────────┐
│        Funeral Participants - Part 1              │
│                    Do You Have                    │
│    Preferred      A Preference? Name/Address/     │
│    Participant       Yes / No     Telephone       │
│    PrimaryClergy to Preside   __ __  _____  │
│    Secondary Clergy to                            │
│    Preside                    __ __  _____  │
│    Casket Bearer              __ __  _____  │
│    Honaray Casket Bearer      __ __  _____  │
│                                                   │
└─────────────────────────────────────────────────┘
```

- Primary/Secondary Clergy to Preside/Church: Place a check mark beneath 'yes' or 'no' and the full name of each clergy member, address (including city, state and zip code) and their telephone number with area code.

- Casket Bearer: Place a check mark beneath 'yes' or 'no' and the full name address (including city, state and zip code) and telephone number with area code for each casket bearer.

- Honorary Casket Bearer: Place a check mark beneath 'yes' or 'no' and the full name address (including city, state and zip code) and telephone number with area code for each honorary casket bearer.

Funeral Participants – Part 2

The *Funeral Participants – Part 2* form is used to record the information about the people that you would like to have speak, read or sing at your funeral ceremony.

In most funeral services there are numerous readings that are either recited by the clergy or the person or persons who have been designated. For each poem, scripture, word of comfort or statement of your life, you will need to list your choice of the persons to whom you would give these different addresses in your *Last Wishes*. Keep in mind that those people that you choose will be grieving, so they may decline the invitation. At least, you will have listed your *Last Wishes* here.

Just as music is an integral part of many people's lives, it is also an integral part of most funeral services. You may like a particular person to sing or play an instrument at your funeral, and vocal accompaniments, organ, piano, violin, bagpipes, are acceptable.

The eulogy is a reflection of the deceased's life. It is suggested that the one designated to give the eulogy speaks about you personally, remembering your life and accomplishments, while offering hope and solace to the surviving family and friends. A person's eulogy is a reflection on and affirmation of their life. A eulogy is a way to proclaim love, help in the healing process, and share the sadness, laughter, joy, and tears.

Funeral Participants – Part 2

Preferred Participant	Do You Have A Preference? Yes / No	Name	Location/ Address / Telephone
Soloist	__ __	_____	_____
Organist	__ __	_____	_____
Pianist	__ __	_____	_____
Bagpiper	__ __	_____	_____
Reader	__ __	_____	_____
Reader	__ __	_____	_____
Eulogy	__ __	_____	_____

- Soloist/Organist/Pianist/Bagpiper/Reader/Eulogy Preferred Participants: For each of these people place a check mark beneath 'yes' or 'no' and name, address (including street, city, state and zip code) and their telephone number.

Requested Musical Selections

The *Requested Musical Selection* form is used to record the music for the funeral ceremony. Music affects our feelings and the atmosphere in which we pray. It expresses our inner thoughts and brings our emotions to the surface. Music for the church funeral service should be selected on the basis of its appropriateness for worship. Of all types of music available for the funeral service, congregational hymns are the most fitting and meaningful. Hymns already familiar to the bereaved take on an added dimension when sung or played for the funeral.

Your favorite music can be played during the service and or highlighted at special times. The funeral participants may sing hymns or songs together or a soloist might perform a particular selection requested by you. Music for the funeral reflects many moods. It may express sorrow and joy, or maybe meditative or triumphant in tone; throughout the funeral choose music and songs to set a mood. In addition, you may want to pick some of your favorite popular tunes to be performed at your funeral service. Musical numbers can consist of voice (soloist or choir), instrumental (piano, harp, flute, organ, guitar, violin or bagpipes, etc.) or recorded music.

In the Appendix of this manual we have included many selections of hymns, as well as classical and popular tunes that may be appropriate for a funeral.

Requested Musical Selections					
Name Of Song Or Hymn	Original Artist Music	The Type of Instrument to Be Used			
		Vocal	Organ	Harp	Other
___	___	___	___	___	___
___	___	___	___	___	___

- Name of Song or Hymn: Include the name of each song or hymn, the original artist for popular songs, and the type of musical instrument for the arrangement.

Requested Reading Selections

The *Requested Reading Selections* form is used to record the various readings that may be included in your funeral service.

In the Appendix of this manual many selections are included from the Old Testament, New Testament and other parts of the Bible.

Recommended Reading Selections

Name   Book   Author   Reference

- Recommended Reading Selections: Include the proper name, book, reference and author for each reading that you have chosen.

Family Medical History

The *Family Medical History* forms is used for recording your family's medical history. This form will be beneficial to your descendants.

Hereditary traits and genetics play an important part in diagnosing and treating many diseases and ailments. One new direction that this has taken is in the form of cryo-preservation of DNA to assure your descendants that they will have your genetic information in the future. For more information please refer to the appendix.

Family Medical History

Problem	Self	Mother	Father	Maternal Grandmother	Maternal Grandfather	Paternal Grandmother	Paternal Grandfather
Birthplace							
Alcoholism							
Allergies							
Back Problems							
Blood							
Bones (where)							
Cancer (where)							
Diabetes							
Digestive System							
Drug Sensitivities							
Eye Disorder							
Hearing Disorder							
Heart Disorder							
Kidney Disorder							
Liver Disorder							
Mental Disorder							
Muscle							
Nerve							
Reproductive							
Respiratory							
Skeletal							
Stroke							
Urinary Problems							
Other Problems							
Major Surgery							
Age at Death							
Cause of Death							

- For all entries: Place a check mark if applicable or insert the name of the specific medical problem into the appropriate space provided.

FAMILY TREE

The *Family Tree* form is used to record the names of your ancestors. This form has been included to assist you in documenting your heritage. Please use this form to provide information that your descendants may not have.

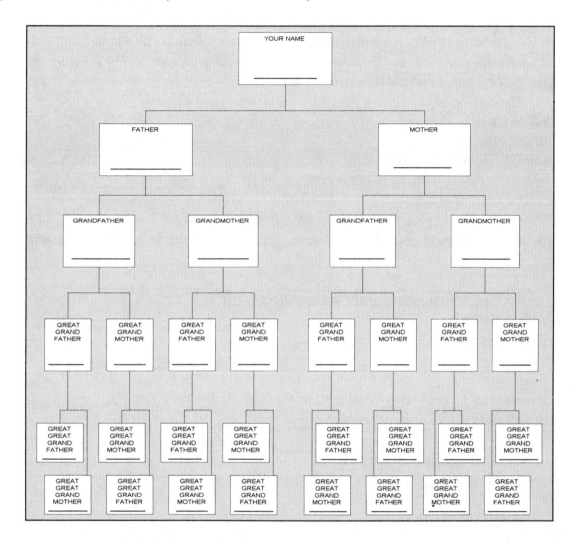

- For each space enter the appropriate name, dates and place of birth to complete the form.

If you have made it this far and filled out the forms as you went along, then you are finished with your *Last Wishes*. Put this in a safe place. A place where you can get to it easily so you can update your information, or periodically review your choices as time goes on.

APPENDIX 1
Business, Professional, and Consumer Groups

American Association of Retired Persons (AARP)
AARP Fulfillment
601 E. Street, N.W.
Washington, D.C. 20049
(800) 424-3410   http:/www.aarp.com

The AARP is a non-profit, nonpartisan organization dedicated to helping older Americans achieve lives of independence, dignity and purpose. They offer many publications and resources about funerals, death, dying.

American Red Cross
431 18th Street, NW
Washington, DC 20006
(202) 639-3520 or (800) Help-Now (to donate organs)   http:/www.redcross.org

The Red Cross is the largest supplier of blood, plasma, and tissue products. Their publications and information can assist with any type of organ or tissue donation questions.

Association for Death Education and Counseling (ADEC)
342 North Main Street
West Hartford, Connecticut 06117-2507
(860) 586-7503   http:/www.adec.org

ADEC is committed to providing a place for the knowledge and practical applications associated with the subject of death and dying.

Counsel of Better Business Bureau (BBB)
4200 Wilson Boulevard
Suite 800
Arlington, Virginia 22203-1838
(703) 247-9357   http:/www.bbb.org

The BBB provides a wide variety of helpful publications, information and resources to both consumers and businesses.

Consumer Federation of America Foundation (CFAF)
1424 16th Street, NW
Washington, DC 20036
(202) 387-6121   http:/www.consumerfed.org

The CFAF provides information to the public on consumer issues.

APPENDIX 1
Business, Professional, and Consumer Groups

Consumer Law Page
Alexander, Hawes & Audet, LLP
152 North 3rd Street
Suite 600
San Jose, CA 95112
(408) 289-1776   http://consumerlawpage.com

The Consumer Law Page is an internet site that provides practical legal info for public consumers.

Cremation Association of North America (CANA)
401 North Michigan Avenue
Chicago, Illinois 60611
(312) 544-6610   http:/www.cremationassociation.org

CANA is an association of crematories, crematories, and funeral homes that offer cremation. More than 750 members own and operate crematories and encourage the concept of memorialization.

Department of Veterans Affairs (VA)
810 Vermont Ave. NW
Washington, DC 20420
(202) 273-5400   http:/www.va.gov

The VA is the government agency that administers the laws providing benefits and other services to veterans and their dependents and the beneficiaries of veterans. The VA ensures that veterans receive medical care, benefits, social support, and lasting memorials promoting the health, welfare, and dignity of all veterans in recognition of their service to this Nation.

Families USA
1334 G Street, NW
Third Floor
Washington, DC 20005-3169
(202) 628-3030   http:/www.familiesusa.org

Families USA is a non-profit organization dedicated to high quality affordable health and long term care. They offer many publications for consumer and seniors.

Federal Consumer Information Center (FCIC)
Department WWW
Pueblo, CO 81009
1-888-878-3256   http:/www.fcic.gov

The FCIC is a government agency that helps other government agencies and departments to develop and distribute useful consumer information to the public.

Federal Information Center (FIC)
1-800-688-9889   http:/www.fic.gov

FIC is a government funded group that has extensive amounts of information about the Federal Government and its associated agencies and programs.

Federal Trade Commission (FTC)
600 Pennsylvania Avenue, NW
Washington, DC 20580
(877) 382-4357   http:/www.ftc.gov

The FTC publishes free brochures on many consumer issues including funerals and funeral related issues,

Funeral and Memorial Societies of America - Funeral Consumers Alliance (FAMSA-FCA)
P.O. Box 10
Hinesbug, VT 05461
1-800-458-5563   http:/www.funerals.org

FAMSA-FCA is a consumer organization that disseminates information about alternatives for funeral or non-funeral dispositions. It encourages advanced planning and cost efficiency.

Funeral Service Consumer Assistance Program (FSCAP)
National Research and Information Center
2250 E. Devon Avenue, Suite 250
Des Plaines, Illinois 60018
(800) 662-7666

FSCAP is a program designed to help consumers and funeral directors resolve disagreements about funeral service contracts. FSCAP is a service of the National Research and Information Center, an independent, nonprofit organization that researches and provides consumer information on death, grief, and funeral service.

APPENDIX 1
Business, Professional, and Consumer Groups

Health Resources and Services Administration (HRSA)
5600 Fishers Lane
Rockville, Maryland 20857
(301) 443-3300   http:/www.hrsa.gov

The HRSA provides federal oversight for the nation's organ procurement, allocation, and transplantation system. They offer publications and further information about organ donations.

International Order of the Golden Rule (OGR)
P.O. Box 3586
Springfield, Illinois 62708
(217) 793-3322   http:/www.ogr.org

OGR is an international association of independent funeral homes.

Jewish Funeral Directors Association (JFDA)
Seaport Landing
150 Lynnway, Suite 506
Lynn, Massachusetts 09102
(617) 477-9300   http:/www.jfda.com

JFDA is a national trade association of funeral directors serving the Jewish community.

National Hospice Organization (NHO)
1901 North Fort Myers Drive
Suite # 307
Arlington, VA 22209
(703) 243-5900   http:/www.nho.org

NHO offers information on hospices and terminally-ill patient providers.

National Kidney Foundation (NKF)
30 East 33rd. Street
New York, New York 10016
(800) 622-9010   http:/www.kidney.org

The NKF is a voluntary health organization that seeks to prevent kidney and urinary tract diseases with information for organ and tissue donors and recipients.

National Funeral Directors Association (NFDA)
13625 Bishops Drive
Brookfield, Wisconsin 53005
(800) 228-6332   http:/www.nfda.org

The NFDA is a funeral service organization that assists funeral directors to provide better service to consumers through education and a code of ethics.

National Funeral Directors and Morticians Association (NFDAM)
3951 Snapfinger Parkway, Suite 570
Decatur, Georgia 30035
(404) 286-6680 or (800) 434-0958   http:/www.nfdma.com

NFDMA is a national association of primarily African-American funeral providers.

National Selected Morticians (NSM)
5 Revere Drive, Suite 340
Northbrook, Illinois 60062-8009
(847) 559-9569   http:/www.nsm.com

NSM is a national association of funeral firms in which membership is by invitation only and conditioned upon the commitment of each firm to comply with the association's Code of Good Funeral Practice.

United Network for Organ Sharing (UNOS)
1100 Boulders Parkway
Richmond, Virginia 23225
(804) 330-8541   http:/www.unos.org

UNOS is a private not-for-profit organization that administers the national Organ Procurement Network (OPTN) for organ transplantation. They offer information on organ donation.

Veterans Benefit Administration (VBA)
1120 Vermont Ave. NW
Washington, DC 20421
(800) 827-1000   http:/www.vba.va.gov

The VBA provides benefits and services to veterans and their families in a responsive, timely and compassionate manner in recognition of their service to the Nation.

APPENDIX 2
Biblical Readings

Readings from the Old Testament

☐ Daniel   12:1-3
Those who lie sleeping in the dust will awake.

☐ Isaiah   25:6-9
He will swallow up death forever.

☐ Isaiah   6:1-3
To comfort those who mourn.

☐ Lamentations   3:17-26
It is good to hope in silence for the Lord God to save.

☐ Lamentations   3:22-26, 31-33
The Lord is good to those who wait for him.

☐ Wisdom   4:7-15
For the just man, though he died early, he shall be at rest.

☐ Job   19:21-27a
The hand of God has struck me.

Readings from the New Testament

☐ Acts   10:34-43
God has appointed Jesus to judge everyone, alive and dead.

☐ Romans   5:17-21
Where sin increased, the grace abounded all the more.

☐ Romans   6:3-9
Let us walk in newness of life.

☐ Romans   14:7-12
Whether alive or dead, we belong to the Lord.

☐ I Corinthians   15:51-57
Death is swallowed up in victory.

☐ II Corinthians   4:16-5:9
Things that are unseen last forever.

☐ I John   3:14-16
We have passed from death to life.

☐ Revelation   7:9-17
God will wipe away every tear.

☐ Revelation   14:13
Happy are those who die in the Lord.

☐ Revelation   20:11-21:1
The dead have been judged according to their conduct.

☐ Revelation   21:2-7
Behold, I make all things new.

☐ I Thessalonians 4:13-18
Those who have died in Christ will rise first.

☐   II Timothy   2:8-13
If we have died with him, then we shall live with him.

Readings from the Gospel

☐   John   5:24-29
He who believes has everlasting life.

☐   John   6:37-40
All that the Father gives me will come to me.

☐   John   6:51-59
All who eat this bread will live forever; and I will raise them up on the last day.

☐   John   10:11-16
I am the good shepherd.

☐   John   11:21-27
I am the resurrection and the life.

☐   John   11:32-45
Lazarus, come out.

☐   John   12:23-28
If a grain of wheat falls on the ground and dies, it yields a rich harvest.

☐   John   14:1-6
There are many rooms in my Father's house.

☐   John   17:24-25
Father, I want those who have given me to be with me where I am.

☐   John   19:17-18, 25-30
Jesus bowed his head and gave up his spirit.

☐   Matthew   5:1-12a
Rejoice and be glad, for your reward will be great in heaven.

☐   Matthew   11:25-30
Come to me...and I will give you rest.

☐   Matthew   25:31-46
Come, you whom my Father has blessed.

☐   Mark   15:33-39, 16:1-6
Jesus gave a loud cry and breathed his last.

☐   Luke   7:11-17
Young man, I say to you, arise.

☐   Luke   12:35-40
Be prepared.

☐   Luke   23:44-46, 50, 52-53
Father, I put my life in your hands.

☐   Psalm 23   1-4
The Lord is my shepherd I shall not want.

☐   Psalm 73   23-26
You have hold of my right hand.

Flowers

Name	Color	Meaning
Alstroemeria	All Colors	Strength, devotion
Aster	All Colors	Virtue
Azalea	All Colors	Temperance
Carnation	All Colors	Joy
Carnation	White	Pure love or remember me
Carnation	Pink	Women's love
Carnation	Green	St. Patrick's Day
Carnation	Purple	Capriciousness
Carnation	Red	I love you
Chrysanthemum	All Colors	Hope
Chrysanthemum	Red	Remember me or I love you
Chrysanthemum	White	Fidelity, truth
Chrysanthemum	Yellow	I'm sorry or I'm sad
Daffodil	All Colors	Respect
Daffodil	Yellow	Chivalry
Fern	All Colors	Grace
Gladiolus	All Colors	Remembrance
Huckleberry	All Colors	Faith
Iris	All Colors	Promise
Larkspur	All Colors	Appreciation
Liatris	All Colors	Gladness
Lily	All Colors	Devotion
Lily	White	Purity, virginity or sweetness
Lily	Yellow	Gratitude / gaiety
Orchid	All Colors	Thoughtfulness and wisdom
Poinsettia	All Colors	Mirth
Snapdragon	All Colors	Intrigue
Rose	All Colors	Love
Rose	Red	True love and desire
Rose	White	Spiritual and true love
Rose	White	I'm worthy of you
Rose	Black	Farewell, death
Rose	Yellow	Friendship
Rose	Pink	Sweetness, please believe me
Rose	White & Red	Unity
Tulip	All Colors	Luck
Tulip	Red	Declaration of love
Tulip	Yellow	Hopelessly in love, purity
Violet	Violet	Virtue

APPENDIX 4
Musical Selections - Secular

Organ preludes and postludes
- ☐ A Lovely Rose Is Blooming
- ☐ Adagio *from* The First Organ Sonata
- ☐ Adagio *from* Toccata
- ☐ Adorn Thyself, O My Soul
- ☐ Andanta *from* Grande Piece Symphonique
- ☐ Communion
- ☐ Deck Thyself, My Soul Funeral March and Song of the Seraphs
- ☐ Hark, A Voice Saith, All Is Mortal
- ☐ He, Remembering His Great Mercy
- ☐ O God, Have Mercy
- ☐ O God, Thou Faithful God
- ☐ O Sacred Head Now Wounded
- ☐ Our Father, Thou Art In Heaven
- ☐ Prayer and Cradle Song
- ☐ Prelude In Olden Style
- ☐ Rejoice Greatly, O My Soul

For Congregational, Choral, or Solo Singing
- ☐ Abide With Me
- ☐ All Creatures Of Our God And King
- ☐ At The Lamb's High Feast
- ☐ Be Not Afraid
- ☐ Because The Lord Is My Shepherd
- ☐ Behold the Lamb
- ☐ Beneath The Cross of Jesus
- ☐ Blest Are They
- ☐ Blest Be the Everlasting God
- ☐ Brief Life Is Here Our Portion
- ☐ Center Of My Life
- ☐ Christ Is Our Light
- ☐ Christ the Lord Is Risen Today
- ☐ Christ The Victorious
- ☐ Come To Me
- ☐ Come Ye, Disconsolate
- ☐ Come, O Thou Traveler Unknown
- ☐ Crown Him with Many Crowns
- ☐ Day Is Done
- ☐ Dear Lord And Father Of Mankind

- ☐ Eat This Bread
- ☐ Eye Has Not Seen Only In God
- ☐ Farewell Blessings
- ☐ Around The Throne Of God
- ☐ Christ, The Way, The Truth, The Life
- ☐ Come, Thou Fount Of Every Blessing
- ☐ For All the Saints
- ☐ Gentle Shepherd
- ☐ Gift Of the Finest Wheat
- ☐ Give Them Rest
- ☐ God Of Day And God of Darkness
- ☐ God Of The Living
- ☐ Great Is Thy Faithfulness

For Congregational, Choral, or Solo Singing
- ☐ Guide Me, O Thou Great Jehovah
- ☐ Hark! Hark, My Soul! Angelic Songs
- ☐ He Leadeth Me
- ☐ Hold Me In Life
- ☐ How Blest Are They
- ☐ How Firm A Foundation
- ☐ How Great Thou Art
- ☐ How Lovely Is Your Dwelling Place
- ☐ I Am the Bread of Life
- ☐ I Am the Living Bread
- ☐ I Am the Resurrection
- ☐ I Have Seen the Lord
- ☐ I Heard the Voice of Jesus
- ☐ I Know That My Redeemer Lives
- ☐ I Lift Up My Soul
- ☐ I Will Lift Up My Eyes
- ☐ I Will Not Die
- ☐ I Will Praise You, Lord
- ☐ In The Breaking Of The Bread
- ☐ In The Hour of Trial
- ☐ Jerusalem The Golden
- ☐ Jerusalem, My Happy Home
- ☐ Jesus, Lord Have Mercy
- ☐ Jesus, Lover of My Soul
- ☐ Jesus, Remember Me
- ☐ Keep In Mind
- ☐ Lead, Kindly Light

☐ Let Saints On Earth In Concert Sing
☐ Like A Child Rests
☐ Lord of the Living
☐ Love Divine, All Loves Excelling
☐ May Saints and Angels
☐ My Faith Looks Up To Thee
☐ My Shepherd Will Supply My Need
☐ My Shepherd, Lord
☐ My Soul Rejoices
☐ Now Thank We All Our God
☐ Now the Laborer's Task Is Over
☐ O God of Bethel, By Whose Hand
☐ O God, For You I Long
☐ O God, Our Help In Ages Past
☐ O Jesus, I Have Promised
☐ O Lord Of Life
☐ O Lord, I Will Sing
☐ O Love That Will Not Let Me Go
☐ O Master, Let Me Walk With Thee
☐ O Mother Day, Jerusalem
☐ On Eagle's Wing
☐ On Our Journey To The Kingdom
☐ One Sweetly Solemn Thought
☐ Our God, Our Help in Ages Past
☐ Out Of Darkness
☐ Out Of the Depths
☐ Remember Your Love
☐ Rock Of Ages
☐ Savior, Like A Shepherd Lead Us
☐ Shelter Me, O God
☐ Shepherd Of Souls
☐ Sing A New Song
☐ Sing With All the Saints In Glory
☐ Softly And Tenderly Jesus Is Calling
☐ Song of Farewell
☐ Songs of the Angels
☐ Sunset and Evening Star
☐ Taste And See
☐ Ten Thousand Times Ten Thousand
☐ The Cry of the Poor
☐ The King Of Love My Shepherd Is
☐ The Lord Is My Hope
☐ The Lord Is Near

☐ The Lord's My Shepherd, I'll Not
   Want
☐ The Old Rugged Cross
☐ There is A Green Hill Far Away
☐ This Alone
☐ This Day in New Jerusalem
☐ Through The Mountains May Fall
☐ To Jesus Christ, Our Sovereign King
☐ Unless A Grain Of Wheat
☐ Unto The Hills Around Do I Lift Up
☐ We Walk By Faith
☐ We Will Rise Again
☐ What a Friend We Have In Jesus
☐ What Their Joy And Their Glory
   Must Be
☐ What Wondrous Love Is This
☐ When I Survey The Wondrous Cross
☐ Yes, I Shall Arise
☐ You Are My God
☐ You Are Near
☐ You Know Me, Lord

CHORAL ANTHEMS
☐ Ah, How Fleeting
☐ Blest Are the Departed
☐ Cain-O Blest Are They
☐ Crossing The Bar
☐ Forever Blest Are They
☐ Forever With the Lord
☐ God So Loved the World
☐ Great and Marvelous
☐ Happy And Blest Are They
☐ He Shall Endure To the End
☐ I Heard A Voice Heaven
☐ Jesus, Friend of Sinners
☐ Lo, My Shepherd Is Divine
☐ My Hope Is In The Everlasting
☐ No Shadows Yonder
☐ Now Let Every Tongue Adore Thee
☐ Now the Day Is Over
☐ The Lord Is My Light
☐ The Souls of the Righteous
☐ Unfold, Ye Portals Everlasting

APPENDIX 5
Musical Selections - Non-Secular

Classical Passages

- ☐ Adagio for Strings - composed by Samuel Barber
- ☐ Air from Suite in D – composed by Bach
- ☐ Ava Maria - composed by Franz Schubert
- ☐ Carnival of The Animals (The Swan) – composed by Saint-Saens
- ☐ Cello Concerto in E minor (Op 85, 3rd movement) - composed by Edward Elgar
- ☐ Etude in E minor (Tristesse)– composed by Chopin
- ☐ Fanfare for the Common Man - composed by Aaron Copeland
- ☐ Funeral March of a Marionette - composed by Gounod
- ☐ Moonlight Sonata (Adagio) – composed by Beethoven
- ☐ Nocturne in E Minor (Op 72) - composed by Chopin
- ☐ Pavane Pour Une Infante Defunte - composed by Maurice Ravel
- ☐ Prelude in C Minor (Op 28, #20) - composed by Chopin
- ☐ Prelude # 4 – composed by Chopin
- ☐ Requiem - composed by Mozart
- ☐ Kinderszenen (Dreaming) – composed by Schumann
- ☐ String Quartet No 2 (Notturno) – composed by Borodin
- ☐ Swan of Tuonela (Op22, # 3) - composed by Jean Sibelius
- ☐ Taps - composer unknown
- ☐ Theme From Paganini – composed by Rachmaninov
- ☐ Toccatta in D - composed by J. S. Bach
- ☐ Violin Concerto in G Minor (# 1) - composed by Max Bruch

Popular Tunes

- ☐ Angel - performed by Sarah McLachlan
- ☐ Bluer Than Blue – performed by Michael Johnson
- ☐ Because You Loved Me - performed by Celine Dion
- ☐ Bridge Over Troubled Water - performed by Simon and Garfunkel
- ☐ Candle In The Wind - performed by Elton John
- ☐ Change The World - performed by Eric Clapton
- ☐ Dream A Little Dream For Me - performed by the Mamas and the Papas
- ☐ Funeral For A Friend - performed by Elton John
- ☐ Go Rest High On That Mountain - performed by Vince Gill
- ☐ Hero - performed by Mariah Carey
- ☐ Hey Jude - performed by the Beatles
- ☐ How Am I Suppose To Live Without You – performed by Laura Branigan or Michael Bolton
- ☐ How Do I Live - performed by Trisha Yearwood
- ☐ In Heaven There Is No Beer - performed by Cleen Lining
- ☐ Long And Winding Road - performed by the Beatles
- ☐ Miss You Like Crazy – performed by Natalie Cole

Musical Selections - Non-Secular

- ☐ My Father Eyes - performed by Eric Clapton
- ☐ My Way - performed by Frank Sinatra
- ☐ Now and Forever - performed by Carole King
- ☐ Prayer For The Dying - performed by Seal
- ☐ Prop Me Up Beside The Jukebox If I Die - performed by Joe Diffie
- ☐ Reach - performed by Gloria Estafon
- ☐ Still – performed by the Commodores
- ☐ Tears In Heaven - performed by Eric Clapton
- ☐ The Sound of Silence - performed by Simon and Garfunkel
- ☐ The Way We Were - performed by Barbra Streisand
- ☐ Time In A Bottle – performed by Jim Croce
- ☐ The Living Years - performed by Mike and the Mechanics
- ☐ Un-Break My Heart - performed by Toni Braxton
- ☐ Wind Beneath My Wings - performed by Bette Midler
- ☐ Yesterday - performed by the Beatles
- ☐ You Are Not Alone - performed by Michael Jackson
- ☐ You Can't Always Get What You Want - performed by The Rolling Stones

Broadway and Show Tunes

- ☐ People - from "Funny Girl" by Jule Styne
- ☐ Phantom of The Opera - from "The Phantom of The Opera" by Andrew Lloyd Webber
- ☐ Memory - from "Cats" by Andrew Lloyd Webber
- ☐ No One Is Alone - from "Into The Woods" by Stephen Soundheim
- ☐ Somewhere - from "West Side Story" by Leonard Bernstein

Movie Themes and Related Music

- ☐ A Time For Us - from the movie: "Romeo and Juliet"
- ☐ Days of Wine and Roses - from the movie: "Days of Wine and Roses"
- ☐ Lara's Theme - from the movie: "Dr. Zhivago"
- ☐ Love Story Theme – from the movie: "Love Story"
- ☐ On Golden Pond Theme - from the movie: "On Golden Pond"
- ☐ Summer of 42 Theme – from the movie: "Summer of 42"
- ☐ The Impossible Dream (The Quest) - from the movie: "Don Quixote"
- ☐ Theme From Mash - from the movie: "MASH"

Arrangement Conference

An arrangement conference is the meeting with the funeral director and family during which choices of the services and merchandise are made.

Basic Arrangements Fee

This charge is determined by the funeral home for making all the arrangements associated with final disposition of the body. The fee includes compensation for the funeral director, staff, arrangement conference, and obtaining necessary authorizations for filing the death certificate and obtaining permits.

Body Donation

A body donation is a personal choice to have one's body donated to science for research purposes.

Burial

Burial is the most common final disposition of the remains of the deceased body into the ground.

Cash Advance Items

The items of service or merchandise are those which the funeral home pays directly to a third party, such as fees for the cemetery or crematory, death certificates and clergy.

Casket

A casket is the common name for a suitable burial container for the deceased body. It always consists of four sides, while styles, sizes, and prices vary considerably.

Casket Bearer

A casket bearer is a person who has been selected to carry the coffin or casket from the funeral service to the hearse and to the burial site.

Casket Price List

The casket price list is a printed or typewritten list, which the funeral home presents to the consumer before discussing and showing a casket.

Cemetery Deed

The cemetery deed is the official document secured from the cemetery that establishes the right to bury the deceased in a designated plot.

Coffin

A coffin is a six-sided container that is usually constructed of wood. It is wider at the shoulders and tapers for the feet at the opposite end.

Columbarium

A columbarium is a type of vault with spaces for storing urns containing ashes or cremains.

Committal Service

A committal service is the ceremony that is held at the graveside immediately before burial. In the case of cremation, the committal service can be held in the crematory's chapel prior to cremation.

Cremation

Cremation is a process for the final disposition of the remains of deceased, which reduces the body to ashes (cremains).

Crypt

The crypt is a chamber that is wholly or partially under ground or in a mausoleum.

Custodial Fee

The custodial fee may be charged by the funeral home for the days that a body is held and no other services are being provided.

Customer's Designation of Intentions

The designation of intentions is a specific form completed by the funeral director for cremation.

Direct Burial

Direct burial is the final disposition of human remains by burial without a formal viewing, visitation, or ceremony, except for a gravesite service.

Direct Cremation

Direct cremation is the disposition of human remains by cremation without a formal viewing, visitation, or ceremony.

Embalming

The embalming process disinfects, preserves and restores the dead human body to an acceptable physical appearance.

Entombment

Entombment is a burial in a crypt above ground in a mausoleum or a lawn crypt.

Epitaph

An epitaph is an inscription on or at a tomb or a grave in memory of the one buried there.

Eulogy

A eulogy is generally read at the end of a funeral in which the deceased is commended. It may be given by clergy, a close family member or friend. It is a reflection of the life lived and affirms the person's life.

Executor

The executor is the person designated by the deceased to administer the terms of the will.

Funeral Director

The funeral director is the licensed operator of the funeral home.

Funeral Home

The funeral home is a business that specializes in the handling and burial of the remains of the dead.

Funeral Service

A funeral service is a ceremony that is conducted when the deceased person's body is present.

General Price List

This form, lists the price (or range of prices) for all of the services and merchandise regularly offered by the funeral home.

Gift To Science

A gift to science is a body and/or organ donation for medical and dental teaching, research, and transplants.

Grave Liners

A grave liner is an outer burial container that holds the casket to keep the ground from settling.

Hearse

A hearse is a vehicle used to transport the deceased's body.

Itemized Statement of Services

An itemized statement of services is a detailed outline of specific goods and services chosen from the funeral director and includes the price of each item and the total cost.

Living Will

The living will is a legal indication of specific life sustaining measures which may and or may not be taken in the event of incapacitation or severe illness.

Living Trust
A living trust is a formal arrangement for the transfer of assets from one person to another.

Medical Power of Attorney
The medical power of attorney is a legal document appointing another person to make health-related decisions for one unable to communicate those decisions.

Memorial Gifts
Memorial gifts are given to charitable institutions in the memory of the deceased.

Memorial Park
A memorial park offers a place to remember the deceased, but the remains are placed elsewhere.

Memorial Service
A memorial service is a ceremony conducted without the presence of the body.

Military Funeral
A military funeral is a ceremony arranged by the military and may include a band, military escorts, caissons, colors, firing squad, uniformed pallbearers, and the playing of taps.

Mortician
A mortician is the licensed professional who prepares the dead for burial.

Obituary
An obituary is a public announcement traditionally found in a newspaper informing the public of a person's death.

Organ Donation
An organ donation program is one in which the participant elects to donate vital organs at death to save another's life. Organ donation is a gift of life or sight to the recipient.

Outer Interment Receptacle
An outer interment receptacle is a container in the ground where the casket is placed. Vaults and grave liners are typical examples.

Pall
A pall is a cloth used to cover or drape the casket.

Pallbearers

Pallbearers are persons who have been selected to carry the coffin or casket from the funeral service to the hearse and to the burial site.

Power of Attorney

A power of attorney is a legal document which designates someone duly appointed to act on your behalf.

Refrigeration Fee

Refrigeration fee is the amount charged by some funeral homes for cooling a body when embalming is declined.

Topical Disinfection

Topical disinfection is an external cleaning of the body.

Transfer of Remains Fee

Transfer of remains fee is a transportation fee to move the body from the place where death occurred to the funeral home.

Urn

An urn is a conveniently sized, sealed container for storing the cremated remains of a human body.

Vault

A vault is an outer burial container that completely encloses a casket in the ground.

Viewing

A viewing is a scheduled time when the deceased is presented to the general public; the casket may be open or closed.

Visitation

A visitation is a scheduled time when the deceased is presented so family and friends can pay their final respects.

Wake

A wake is service held before a funeral ceremony during which friends and relatives can visit and pay their final respects.

Will

A will (Last Will and Testament) is a legal document that specifies how your assets are to be distributed upon your death.

Your

Last Wishes

Forms

NAME:_____

DATE COMPLETED:_____

REVISED ON:_____

REVISED ON:_____

REVISED ON:_____

REVISED ON:_____

General Information

Full Name:_____

Nick Name:_____

Maiden Name:_____

Date of Birth:_____

Place of Birth:_____

Social Security Number:____-____-____

Marital Status

☐ Single ☐ Married ☐ Divorced

☐ Widow ☐ Widower

Current Marriage

Date: _____ Place: _____

Previous Marriages

Date: _____ Place: _____
Date: _____ Place: _____
Date: _____ Place: _____

Religious Information

Religion: _____

Church Name: _____

Church Address: _____

_____

_____

_____

Telephone: _____

Priest/Minister: _____

Veteran Information

Service / Branch: _____

Date and Place of Enlistment: _____

_____

Date of Discharge: _____

Rank and Service Number: _____

Veterans' Administration Claim #

_____

War / Conflicts / Tours of Duty: _____

_____

Commendations Received: _____

Immediate Family
For use in Notification and Obituary

Relation-ship	Name	Date of Birth	City / State	Telephone
Spouse				
Parent				
Parent				
Child				
Child				
Child				
Child				
Grand-Child				
Grand-Child				
Grand-Child				
Grand-Child				

Immediate Family

For use in Notification and Obituary

Relation-ship	Name	Date of Birth	City / State	Telephone
Sibling				
Sibling				
Sibling				

Membership in Professional, Union, & Fraternal Organizations

For Use in Notification and Obituary

Name	Address	Telephone	Dates

Community and Voluntary Services

For use in Notification and Obituary

Name	Address	Telephone	Dates

Education

For use in Obituary

Type	Name	City / State	Degree	Dates Attended
High School				
Trade School				
College				
Graduate College				
Certificates				

Employers
For use in Obituary

Company	Occupation	Location	Dates

Friends/Employers/ Colleagues

For use in Death Notification

Relation-ship	Name	Date of Birth	City / State	Telephone
Friend				
Friend				
Friend				
Friend				
Friend				
Employer				
Employer				
Employer				
Colleague				
Colleague				
Colleague				

Friends/Employers/ Colleagues (Page 2)

For use in Death Notification

Relation-ship	Name	Date of Birth	City / State	Telephone

Attorney Information

Firm Name:_____

Attorney Name:_____

Address:_____

City / State:_____

Telephone:_____

Executor Information

Name:_____

Address:_____

City / State:_____

Telephone:_____

Documents

Type of Document	Do you Have? Yes/No		Location	Account / Reference #	Other Notes
Will					
Living Will					
Living Trust					
Medical Power of Attorney					
Cemetery Plot Deed					
Safe Deposit Box					
Safe Deposit Box Key					
Automobile Titles					
Birth Certificate					

Documents

Type of Document	Do you Have? Yes/No		Location	Account / Reference #	Other Notes
Passport					
Income Tax Records					
Life Insurance					
Savings Accounts					
Checking Accounts					
Mortgage Papers / Deeds					

Documents

Other Types of Document	Do you Have? Yes/No		Location	Account / Reference #	Other Notes

Newspapers or Publications
For Obituary Notice

Name	Address	Telephone

Final Disposition of Remains

Type	Yes	No
Body Donation for Research		
Cremation		
Burial		

Medical School / Science

Name of School / Organization	Address	Type of Donation
		Corpse
		Vital Organs
		Other Organs

Cremation

Category	Name	Address	Location
Preferred Crematory			
Designation of Intentions			

	Urn	Columbarium	Burial	Scattered
Final Resting Place of Remains				

Burial

Cemetery or Gravesite

Category	Do You have ? Yes/No		Name	Address / Location
Cemetery				
Memorial Park				
Grave Site Purchased				
Grave Deed				
Grave or Niche				
Grave Liner Preference				
Entombment				
Crypt				

Burial Instructions
Clothing or Other Articles

Items	Request Yes/No		Description
Recommended Special Burial Clothes			
Recommended Every Day Burial Clothes			
Other Burial Items			
Other Burial Items			

Burial Instructions
Funeral Home Wishes

Items	Request Yes/No		Name
Designated Contact			
Pre-plan With A Funeral Home?			
Recommended Funeral Home			
Recommended Funeral Director			

Casket Information

Items	Request Yes/No		Description
Casket Purchased			
Casket Preferences			
Metal			
Hardwood			
Pine Box			
Fabric Cover			
Environmental			
Other Style			
Other Preferences			

Gravestones and Monuments

Category	Do You Have Yes/No		Description
Headstone			
Material of Monument			
General Shape of Monument			
General Size of Monument			
Other Monument Preferences			
Epitaph			

Funeral Ceremony Preferences

Type of Preference	Request Yes/No		Description / Name Location
Open Casket			
Closed Casket			
Public			
Private			
In Church			
In Funeral Home			
Other Location			
Memorial Gifts			
In Lieu of Flowers			
Favorite Flowers			
Favorite Flowers			
Favorite Flowers			
Favorite Flowers			

Funeral Participants
Part 1

Preferred Participant	Do You Have Preference? Yes/No	Name	Address / Telephone
Primary Clergy to Preside			
Secondary Clergy to Preside			
Casket Bearer			
Casket Bearer			
Casket Bearer			
Casket Bearer			
Casket Bearer			
Casket Bearer			
Honorary Casket Bearer			

Funeral Participants

Part 2

Preferred Participant	Do You Have Preference? Yes/No		Name	Address / Telephone
Soloist				
Organist				
Pianist				
Bagpiper				
Reader				
Reader				
Reader				
Eulogy				

Self-Written Eulogy

Recommended Musical Selections

Name of Song or Hymn	Original Artist Music	The Type of Instrument to Be Used								Other
		V O C A L	O R G A N	F L U T E	P I A N O	V I O L I N	H A R P	B A G P I P E	G U IT A R	

Recommended Reading Selections

Name	Book	Author	Reference

Family Medical History
Part 1

Problem	Self	Mother	Father	Maternal Grandmother	Maternal Grandfather	Paternal Grandmother	Paternal Grandfather
Birthplace							
Alcoholism							
Allergies							
Blood							
Bones (where)							
Cancer (where)							
Diabetes							
Digestive System							
Drug Sensitivities							
Eye Disorder							
Hearing Disorder							
Heart Disorder							
Kidney Disorder							
Liver Disorder							

Family Medical History
Part 2

Problem	Self	Mother	Father	Maternal Grandmother	Maternal Grandfather	Paternal Grandmother	Paternal Grandfather
Mental Disorder							
Nerve / Muscles							
Reproductive System							
Respiratory System							
Skeletal							
Stroke							
Urinary Problem							
Other							
Other							
Other							
Major Surgery							
Age at Death							
Cause of Death							

Family Tree

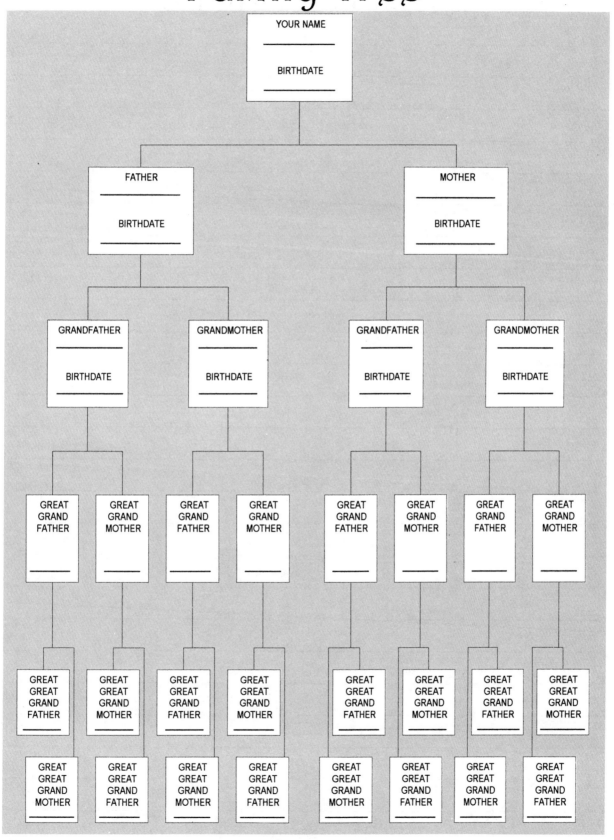

Other Notations